From

HIGH HOUSE

To

BAKER'S OVEN

CW01072956

ROY LEWIS

INTRODUCTION

This book traces the histories of a small group of properties on the western side of Greengate Street. When numbers were allocated to them in 1850, they became numbers 47 to 58. Staffordians may recognise them more readily as being those properties between The High House and The Bakers Oven.

There have been houses on these sites since the middle ages and, perhaps, even earlier, but nothing is known of them. The accounts in this book usually start in the late sixteenth or seventeenth centuries, a few in the early eighteenth century. It is noticeable that, throughout all the rebuilding, sites have remained constant and have shaped the arrangement of this book.

The book was originally published in 2004 as a pilot for a series of books about property and people in the main streets of the town – The Stafford Street Series. It was reprinted in 2004 and is now being published in a second edition with additional information about some of the properties and minor corrections.

The sources used are inevitably incomplete and, before properties were numbered, there is the additional difficulty of identifying properties and those who lived in them. Sources often allow only an approximate date to be given and it is almost inevitable that some dates will be adrift by one or two years

My thanks go to the staffs of the William Salt Library, the Staffordshire County Record Office and the Staffordshire County Library for help and advice, to Mrs Fiona Sheridan for her invaluable contributions to the account of the High House, and to numerous individuals for sharing information and making helpful suggestions.

June 2007

THE HIGH HOUSE (NUMBERS 47 to 49)

The High House was built as a single dwelling but in the early nineteenth century was converted into three shops and is now a museum entered between two shops. The first section of this account relates the story of the High House as a whole down to the time of its conversion. Later sections give separate accounts of the three shops after that date.

The earliest picture of the High House is a drawing made in 1823 by John Robert Ferneyhough, the 15 year old son of Captain Thomas Ferneyhough, who lived in the house from 1823 to 1826. The drawing is now in the William Salt Library (SMS 370i). In 1833 figures were added in the street and the drawing published as a sitograph, or engraving, dedicated to Hugh Henshall Williamson on his appointment as High Sheriff of the county. This is reproduced above. There are two other drawings of the High House by John and Anna Ferneyhough in the William Salt Library.

The High House is an extravagant building. Only a family with considerable wealth could afford to build a town house of this size, with four storeys jettied out over the street, and a plan, like a capital E with its back facing Greengate Street, which incorporated the most up-to-date ideas of the late sixteenth century. Those who built it were not only wealthy but also wanted to display their wealth for all to see, both by the imposing size of their house and by adding expensive, ornate bracing to its timber frame.

For such a prominent building its early history is surprisingly uncertain. Local folklore, first recorded in the early nineteenth century, has it that the timber was felled in Doxey Wood. The beams, sills and studs are said to have been sawn to size and the joints cut and fitted there before the frame was taken apart and brought on site to be re-assembled. Before this, normal sixteenth century building practice would have prepared the site by digging out cellars and lining the walls with stone blocks. These would be extended several feet above ground level to form a plinth for the rest of the house. This was especially necessary to provide a level base on a sloping site like that in Greengate Street, although its main purpose was to keep the timber sills dry. The solid stone and brick chimney stacks would also have been built at this stage, although the fireplaces would be finished later.

The ground floor timber frame would then be assembled on site in sections and hoisted into place with sills resting on the plinth. The joists of the first floor, already cut to size were then pegged into position before frames for the upper floors were hoisted into place, one storey at a time. Later the roof would be tiled, the spaces in the timber frame filled, ornamental bracing added, staircases built in the middle projection of the capital E plan and floor boards laid.

In 1947 an oak plaque with the words THOMAS CLE CARPINDER, DID MAKE THIS HOUSE is said to have been uncovered under plaster at the front of the building. Thomas Clay is recorded as a carpenter in Stafford in the late sixteenth century and was employed during the building of the Shire Hall in the middle of the market place. However, the plaque is not as

2

old as the sixteenth century and there is no evidence to
suggest that it is a replica of an inscription uncovered in
earlier alterations. Its discovery went unrecorded except
in a scribbled note by local historian J.S.Horne (now in
the County Record Office) and little reliance can be placed
on it. The plaque was quickly lost and not rediscovered
until 1961 when it was found among rubbish in a disused
coal shed at The Swan and put on display there. At some
time after 1947 a date 1580 A.D. seems to heve been added
to the plaque.

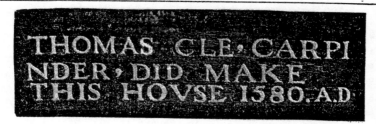

The Thomas Clay plaque rediscovered in February 1961. The
Staffordshire Advertiser suggested it might relate to
work carried out at The Swan.

Other folklore about the High House related that it had
been built for John Dorrington in 1595. This was first written
down in the 1820s by Captain Ferneyhough, but almost certainly
incorporated an older tradition told to him while he was
living in the house. The date fitted the outward appearance
of the building and the Dorringtons were active in local
government in the town at that time so that the tradition was
accepted without question by all who wrote about the High
House. Including William Jones, a local historian who put
together notes about the building about 1870 and then showed
them to James Marson, one of two brothers who owned the High
House.

Marson told him a different story. He said that during
alterations in the late 1820s a discovery had been made. On

a piece of wood, in front of the house, now plastered over, is cut RICHARD DORRINGTON MADE THIS HOUSE, 1555. A few years later, in 1882, William Marson, James' brother, added the information that Mr Carter, the architect, had left a note recording the discovery. Thomas Carter was a builder and joiner living in St Mary's Churchyard about 1830. The note has disappeared and the inscription has not been re-dis covered during later work on the house, although a much later oak panel, bearing Richard Dorrington's name but no date, was discovered in 1947 at the same time as the Thomas Clay panel.

William Jones seems to have spread the new information widely. Almost every account of the High House from 1882 to 1975 accepts the Marsons' account of the origin of the building. In the 1970s the Borough Council bought the High House with the intention of restoring it to its former state as far as possible. They commissioned F.W.D.Charles, an architect who was expert on timber framed buildings, to make a survey of the building. His report in 1975 stated that the house was not as old as 1555. Its plan and a number of construction details suggested about 1595 as a more probable date. He suggested that Thomas Carter had misread a 9 for a 5 - 'such mistakes are not uncommon'. Since Charles' report it has been generally accepted that Richard Dorrington built the High House about 1595.

Several households in sixteenth century Stafford had the surname Dorrington and most of them were probably related to each other. Some christian names occur in several households, making the identification of individuals difficult. However, only three of those with the surname Dorrington might have been wealthy enough to order the building of the High House.

The first of these is John Dorrington, the son of the Robert Dorrington who was buried in St Mary's parish church in Stafford in 1593. John was almost certainly trained as a lawyer. He married into a London family and lived in the parish of St Andrew, Holborn. When he died in 1613 his will shows that he was still the owner of two houses in Stafford, one in the Foregate and the other in Broadeye, which were

left to his widow and their two sons Francis and Richard.
John Dorrington spent all his adult life in London and it
is highly unlikely that he would build a great house in
Stafford with no intention of living in it.

Accounts of the intrigues that accompanied the obtaining
of a new town charter in 1614 and the visit of James I a few
years later in 1617, show that one of the most active members
of the council at that time was Richard Dorrington. His
relationship with other Dorringtons is unclear but he was the
owner of land in Foregate which had once belonged to the
Franciscan friary there. This had been bought by Matthew
Dorrington in 1581 and by the early seventeenth century was
in Richard's possession.   He was town bailiff in 1604 and
mayor under the new charter in 1615. By that time, he was
no longer a young man. In 1617, just before James I visit
to the town, he refused to ride to Preston to observe the
correct behaviour in the presence of the King, saying that he
was too old to undertake such a journey. He probably died in
1627 with no surviving sons. His property in Foregate was
inherited by Dorothy Dorrington, the wife of Sir Richard
Dyott M.P. for Stafford. If Richard Dorrington of the Friary
had owned the High House, it would have been inherited by
Lady Dyott. The fact that she did not inherit the building
makes it unlikely that this Richard Dorrington was the one
who built it.

The most likely builder of the High House is another
Richard Dorrington, a mercer, who was the brother of John
Dorrington of London referred to above. When he was town
bailiff in 1591 he had the town bye-laws collected into one
volume - The Black Book of Stafford - which he presented to
the council. He died comparatively young in 1597, leaving
a widow and a ten year old son Francis. His business,
dealing in cloth and trading in the London cloth halls, was
extensive and as his profits grew he had invested in property
and land.   At the time of his death he owned six houses as
well as the one he lived in, a newly built barn in Broadeye
and various fields and pieces of land in and about the town.
He was rich. His will mentions items such as two silver-gilt
goblets weighing 20 ounces without their covers and a counter-

5

pane for which he had paid £7. This is at a time when the
wages of a craftsman were a shilling a day or less. There
is no proof that Richard Dorrington, mercer, built the High
House but he is the only member of his family wealthy enough
to have done so and is probably to be credited with having
it built.

'The house I now dwell in', mentioned in his will is
probably the High House and the will gives us glimpses of its
interior when it was newly built. Richard himself might have
been seen in a gown trimmed with beech marten fur worn over a
satin doublet. On his fingers would be a gold ring with a
red stone and his gold signet ring with martlets. On the
ground floor, one room was 'the shop', or place of business,
with scales to weigh gold coin and two 'great chests' in
which money, legal documents and other valuables were locked
away. In the absence of banks, there was often a considerable
sum in the house and other money would be lent at interest.
All these transactions were carefully recorded in the
'square book'. On the first floor, the best bedchamber was
furnished with the great bedstead which Richard had bought
from the widow of Francis Rock. This had a truckle bed for
a servant, which could be pushed under the great bed during
the day. The great bed had green curtains and a valance hung
with gilt balls. It was furnished with a feather mattress
down pillows, blankets, sheets, a counterpane that had cost
£7 and a cadow or cover. At the rear of the house were
stables where Richard kept several horses.

After the death of Richard Dorrington, his widow Margaret
carried on her husband's business with the help and advice of
William Moye, a Stafford mercer and close friend of the family,
and Richard's brother John in London. A few years later, she
moved out of the High House and probably took her young son
Francis to live with relatives. The High House was let at some
time before 1606. In that year William Moye, acting as agent
for the heirs of Richard Dorrington, paid the town chamberlains;

For a barn at Broadeye 6d; for a wayne house at the
barn end 4d; for a garden there, being town land 20d;

for the house now in the tenure of Sir Thomas Crompton,
Kt 4½d; for the stone steps at the same house 4d.'
All these are identical to payments, made by Francis Dorrington in the 1620s, which relate to the High House and the barn
and garden at Broadeye which had been inherited from Richard
Dorrington. The house in the tenure of Sir Thomas Crompton
must be the High House.

Sir Thomas Crompton was a judge of the Admiralty Court.
At some time after leaving The High House he bought an estate
at Creswell. He may have been a relation of the Crompton
family who moved from Stafford to Stone Park when they became
wealthy in the sixteenth century. In the seventeenth century
William Crompton of Stone Park had a brother and son named
Thomas but neither of them were ever knighted.

Lady Crompton, Sir Thomas' wife, appears in a minor role
in the history of the town. It was rumoured that she had
tried to arrange a marriage between her daughter and Matthew
Craddock, the leading townsman of the time. He refused and
she never forgave him. In 1613, when the Craddocks were seek-
ing to obtain a new royal charter for the town, which would
make it possible for the wealthier families to exclude the
ordinary burgesses from positions of authority, she was a
focus for opposition. Those opposing the Craddocks met at her
house and organised a petition to the king against the new
charter. A meeting to find a compromise was also held at her
house and had to be adjourned after supporters of the charter
complained that Lady Crompton and her children were making
too much noise for the meeting to continue. By 1619 she was
a widow living at The Swan, Lord Stafford's house in the
market place.

About 1608 Francis Dorrington was old enough to take
charge of his father's business as a mercer. Soon afterwards
he moved back into the High House. He was probably there by
1612, when he contributed to the cost of paving the main
streets of the town. He also became active in the government
of the town. Another Francis Dorrington was also active in
the town's government and held the post of sergeant-at-mace
(a sort of town constable), with only one short break, from
1609 to 1628. The two Francises can be distinguished because

Richard's son was 'a man of great means' and usually given the courtesy title Mr to mark his standing in the town.

Much of his business was with London merchants and cloth halls. In 1613 he was described as 'single and about to go and live in London'. His name is noticeably missing from the early pages of Matthew Craddock's record of town business in 1614/15 (Matthew Craddock's Book of Remembrance, 1614-15, edited by Ann J.Kettle (1994)). However, by December 1614 he was back in Stafford, taking his place as a member of the council and being presented in court for blocking the street with a cart. In April 1615 he was sitting as a Justice of the Peace and in 1617 was chosen as mayor. During his absence from Stafford he seems to have married - there is no record of his marriage in the register of St Mary's parish church - and in July 1615 the couple's first child, a son named Richard, was baptised at St Mary's. By 1622 they had six children and were employing four servants.

Francis was chosen as one of the town's two chamberlains or treasurers and as such opposed Matthew Craddock's expenditure on a great mace for the town and on a room below the Shirehall to keep town records and impress King James I when he visited the town in 1617. He also opposed a loan to fund a presentation to the King. His trade as a mercer often involved riding to London and on one occasion he dashed into a council meeting 'booted and spurred' to warn against further expenditure on the King's visit. He also refused a council request that he ride to Preston to see how that town received the King. He told them that his business did not leave him time for such visits.

He probably continued to live in the High House. In the 1620s and 1630s he was making annual payments to the town because the porch of his house encroached on Greengate Street and also in connection with the barn and garden at Broadeye which he had inherited from his father. He was again chosen as mayor in 1633 and was still living in the town in 1640, when he paid his share of the Subsidy levied by the King. However, he seems to have left Stafford, perhaps for London, soon afterwards and the High House was let.

The tenant was an ex-naval captain, Richard Sneyd, the
fourth son of Ralph Sneyd of Keele Hall. When Charles I and
his nephew Prince Rupert visited Stafford in September 1642
to recruit men and commandeer horses at the beginning of
the Civil War, the High House was thought the most suitable
lodging for the King. Prince Rupert, who had been fighting
on the Continent, wanted to demonstrate the accuracy of the
latest continental pistols. 'Standing in Captain Richard
Sneyd's garden at the high-house there, at about 60 yards
distance, he made a shot at the weather-cock upon the steeple
of the Collegiate Church of St Mary with a screwed horseman's
pistol, and single bullet, which pierced its tail, the hole
plainly appearing to all that were below: which the King then
present judging as a casualty (lucky shot) only, the Prince
presently proved the contrary by a second shot to the same
effect.'

At the beginning of 1643 Stafford became a Royal
garrison but in the following May was taken by Parliamentary
troops and came under military rule. In January 1644 'the
High House of Mr Dorrington in the tenure of Mr Lees'was
requisitioned for the provost marshall to use as a place of
confinement for the better sort of Royalist prisoners. Those
who gave their parole were allowed into the garden provided
they returned to their rooms by 9.30 p.m. and locked their
doors.

After the Parliamentary Committee at Stafford was
disbanded and the Civil War ended, the High House must have
been handed back to Francis Dorrington. He had probably
returned to Stafford, where he died and was buried at St Mary's
in July 1655. It is not known whether he lived in the High
House after his return. When he died, the house was
inherited by his son William, who paid nine pence to the
town chamberlains in 1662 because the porch and stone steps
of the building were still built out into the street. This
payment would have been made annually but records have not
survived for other years.

1662 is the last year in which the Dorrington family

can be linked to the High House. Four years later, when the Hearth Tax was collected, William Dorrington's name does not appear among those charged. The tax was levied on those who occupied a property so this may simply indicate that the house had been let. If that was the case, the tenant has not been identified, although few houses can have had as many hearths; possibly it had been divided. William Dorrington may have owned the house until his death in 1667.

The history of the building in the late seventeenth century is uncertain. Richard Sneyd, who had lived in the High House in 1642, bought a house in Greengate Street from Abraham Fowler about 1681 and lived there until his death in 1684. In his will, the house was left to his daughter Ann, who later married Edward Wettenhall, a clergyman and the son of the Bishop of Cork. When Edward, by then a widower, died in 1733 he left 'my house called the High House in the town of Stafford' to his daughter, another Anne. Was the house inherited by Anne Wettenhall (nee Sneyd) the same house as that inherited by her daughter? If it was, then Abraham Fowler must have bought or inherited the High House from one of the Dorringtons some time after 1662. No evidence has been discovered as to the ownership of the house at this time, although the town chamberlains' accounts show that Dr Edward Wettenhall was making annual payments for a house in the town from 1699 to 1704. Their accounts for other years have not survived.

Edward Wettenhall's daughter Anne, who had inherited the High House, married John Hawkins, the second son of William Hawkins, Prebendary of Winchester, and a grandson of Izaak Walton. The Hawkins family probably owned the house until some time after the death of Anne Hawkins in 1737. They never lived there, although nineteenth century writers like Charles Calvert in his History of Stafford and Guide to the Neighbourhood (1886), ignoring the fact that Izaak had died in 1683, spread the tale that 'Izaak Walton was born and lived many years in this house'.

At the beginning of the eighteenth century, Stafford's town finances were re-organised with the introduction of 'hind hand rents' payable to the chamberlains by the occupiers of most properties and incorporating the annual payments for porches and other encroachments on the street. Payments varied from a few pence to several shillings. Accounts survive from 1729 and those relating to the High House have been identified. They show that in 1729, and probably for some years before that, the house was occupied by Robert Bosville Esq., a gentleman with a country estate at Bianna near Eccleshall. He retired to live on his estate in 1732. The High House was then let to William Perry until 1741 and after that to George Hunt until 1746. From 1746 to 1758 the tenant was Thomas Neville. A poll book of 1747 lists him as a tenant of Mr Crutchley. This suggests that Mr Crutchley may have bought the house from the heirs of Anne Hawkins in the 1740s.

Brooke Crutchley was a well-to-do apothecary. He moved into the High House in 1758 and may have owned it before then. He was the son of John Crutchley, who had died in 1747 during his year of office as mayor, and had married the sister of John Robins, M.P. for the town In those days apothecaries were medical men, almost the equivalent of a general practitioner today. They treated patients and carried out minor surgery as well as dispensing medicines. Crutchley was appointed apothecary to the gaol in 1746 and a few years later was one of a group of county gentlemen who raised a subscription to found an infirmary in the town. When it opened in 1766, he became a member of the board which met weekly to oversee its affairs. He was chosen as mayor in 1774.

By 1758 the High House had been divided into two dwellings. We do not know if Crutchley made the division or whether it had been done before he moved in. Brooke Crutchley and his family occupied the southern and central parts of the building, with its entrance by way of a porch in Greengate Street. A second, smaller dwelling in the north range had its own internal staircase and an entry into St Mary's Gate at the side. From 1758 to 1766 this smaller dwelling was let to Joseph Adams. Samuel Twigg, who had been sworn in as a burgess in January 1766, then moved in and set up in business as a mercer.

During restoration of the building in the 1970s and 80s

11

scraps of wallpaper dating from the mid-eighteenth century were discovered in the part of the building occupied by Brooke Crutchley. These have been carefully preserved and are now displayed in the High House. Most of the papers show stencilled, or block printed, floral designs but on the staircase walls were a series of recessed panels, showing classical figures and romantic landscapes, framed with a variety of papers.

Brooke Crutchley died in 1777, leaving the house to his second wife, Elizabeth. In 1781 she sold it to Thomas Fowler, who had come from York to Stafford to take up an appointment as physician at the Staffordshire General Infirmary in 1778.

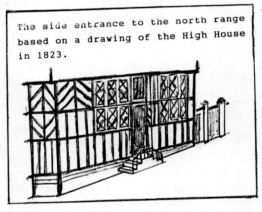

The side entrance to the north range based on a drawing of the High House in 1823.

Thomas Fowler had studied medicine at Edinburgh University and had had a dissertation on the use of mercury in treating patients published in 1778. While living at the High House, he became interested in the effectiveness of Tasteless Ague Drops used to treat patients at the infirmary. He discovered that a small quantity of arsenic was one of the ingredients. He then worked with Richard Hughes, apothecary at the infirmary, to study the effect of small doses of arsenic and to develop Fowler's Solution as a remedy for a variety of ailments. He published his research in 'Medical Reports of the Effect of Arsenic in the Cure of Agues, Remitting Fevers and Periodic Headaches' (1786). Fowler's

Solution was widely used in the treatment of such ailments as epilepsy, cancer, rheumatism, lumbago and asthma. It was also taken by ladies to give their complexion a fashionable pallor. In 1792 Fowler was offered a post as one of the Directors of the York Dispensary, set up to treat the poor of that city. He sold the High House with two cottages and two pews in St Mary's church (one was for servants) for £320 and left Stafford. He later became Chairman of the York Dispensary Board and died in 1801 after a fall from his horse.

The new owner of the High House was another doctor, William Fieldhouse. He had had a practice in Stafford for a number of years and was a member of the council. He was chosen as mayor in 1793, the year in which he moved into the High House. His daughter Jane married Rev Edward Dickenson, who succeeded his father as Rector of St Mary's in 1795. As a doctor he was interested in the benefits of medicinal bathing and installed at the rear of the High House 'a bath so constructed as by its communication with the brewhouse to be made either hot or cold'. Like Thomas Fowler, he lived in the southern part of the house and let the northern range to a succession of tenants - Mr Robinson (1793-6), Mrs Langton, a widow, (1796-7), Mr Henshaw (1798- early 1800s) and Robert Horne. He died in October 1803, in the closing weeks of his second term as mayor, and in 1804 his widow put the house up for sale or to let.

The sale notice described the part of the house that the Fieldhouses occupied as 'a large and commodious messuage well adapted for a large and genteel family'. The accomodation comprised a hall, a shop or consulting room, a breakfast parlour at the front of the house, a dining room with a recess and double doors to the kitchen, a drawing room 19 feet square, six bedrooms, 'all very lofty with large and convenient closets', and a dressing room. The attics were particularly roomy and furnished with lockable wooden bins capable of holding 100 bushels of grain. At the rear of the building was a laundry with drying racks, tables and stoves, a kitchen, two pantries, a brewhouse and a coal house under cover. There were excellent cellars. Outside, was a yard with hogsties, a coach house, a stable for four horses with a hay loft over and a second loft that overhung the passage to the churchyard. The walled garden was 'choicely planted' and had a greenhouse recently erected by Mr Fieldhouse.

The adjoining dwelling at the northern end of the building was included in the sale. It was in the occupation of Robert Horne and comprised a good parlour and kitchen, four spacious lodging rooms (one being used as a sitting room), a brewhouse, a cellar and a pantry.

The property was not sold or let and Mrs Fieldhouse continued to live in it. When Robert Horne moved out, the northern part of the house was let to Dr Gregory, a surgeon and apothecary. He left in April 1806 and a second attempt was then made to sell the High House. This was again unsuccessful.

In 1811 the northern range of the High House was let as a school. The Misses Tomkinson, two unmarried sisters, had opened a small, but select, boarding school for young ladies at Park Lane near Leek in the summer of 1810. The location proved unattractive and the school closed at the beginning of the summer vacation in 1811. It re-opened the following term in the High House, described as 'a commodious house in Greengate Street'.

The Misses Tomkinson advertised that they would adopt 'such parts of the education practiced at the seminary at Ashbourne as are essential to the completion of the female character'. The school was small, probably no more that six or eight young ladies. Fees were 26 guinease a year with a two guinea admission fee. Pupils had to provide a pair of sheets, four napkins, a knife, fork and table spoon. There were additional charges: washing would be done for an extra 16 shillings a quarter and 'tea once a day' cost ½ guinea a quarter. Visiting masters came in to teach additional subjects to those who desired them -geography, writing, French, music, dancing and drawing - all at extra cost. Total fees would probably have been in excess of £50 a year, considerably more than other schools in the town.

After two unsuccessful attempts to sell the main part of the High House, Mrs Fieldhouse (misnamed Mrs Fielden in Pitt's Topographical History of Staffordshire , 1817) carried

on living there herself until the summer of 1822 when she
sold her surplus furniture and moved out. Her part of the
High House was then let to Thomas Ferneyhough, a captain
in the Staffordshire Militia. He had a keen interest in the
history of Staffordshire and in later years compiled and
copied out numerous volumes of local information for William
Salt. These are now housed in the William Salt Library. His
son John Robert and his daughter Anna both made drawings of
the High House which are now bound into these volumes. John
Robert's drawing, made in 1823 when he was 15 years old, was
published in 1833 as a sitograph or engraving which is
reproduced on page one . This is the earliest representation
of the building.

Captain Ferneyhough's wife Sarah had had experience of
running a school for young ladies before she came to Stafford
late in 1822. Soon after she and her husband moved into the
High House, she bought the Misses Tomkinson's school. It
opened under her charge on Ladyday 1823. The whole of the
High House was then occupied by the Ferneyhoughs.

In late 1825, or early 1826, Mrs Fieldhouse managed to
sell the High House. The new owner was Henry Jenkinson, a
hairdresser and perfumier like his father Job. Today, he
would also be described as a property developer, since he
seems to have bought the property with the intention of
developing its commercial potential and then selling it
piecemeal. He gave the Ferneyhoughs notice to close the
school during the summer vacation and to vacate the rest
of the house soon afterwards. An auction sale was held in
July 1826 at which the lots included a pianoforte, school
forms and tables, a pair of 12 inch globes and numerous
books. The pupils of the school had come from families of
good social standing and Mr and Mrs Hudson, who ran a similar
boarding school in Lichfield, made a special offer of free
conveyance to and from Stafford for any of Mrs Ferneyhough's
young ladies who were transferred to their school.

After leaving Stafford, Captain Ferneyhough moved to
Uttoxeter and then Margate before being appointed a Military
Knight at Windsor. In 1841 he became the Governor, or
Commander, of the Knights with a residence 'in one of the

oldest and finest towers of Windsor Castle'. He is buried
in St George's Chapel there.

Henry Jenkinson advertised the property as for sale by
auction at The Swan on 19 February 1827. He described it as
being in a position 'for an extensive wholesale and retail
business where room and publicity are required, such as is
seldom to be met with, and affords any purchaser wishing to
embark on trade an opportunity rarely occurring in the
Borough'. The High House was to be sold in two lots
corresponding to the two dwellings into which it had been
divided since the middle of the eighteenth century. The sale
was cancelled at short notice and a new auction in a single
lot arranged for 3 March. The two sale notices differ in
detail and, in part, complement each other. In between the
two sales Jenkinson changed both the auctioneer and his
solicitor. At the same time as the second auction was
announced, advertisements were placed offering parts of the
property to let from Lady Day (25 March). This may have been
a precaution in case the premises failed to sell at auction.

Lot 1 was what had formerly been the smaller dwelling
with frontages both to Greengate Street and St Mary's Gate.
In the auction notice, it is described as 'a messuage and
shop lately converted out of a dwelling house.' The shop was
39 feet by 19 feet and 'exceptionally lofty with a warehouse
underneath of similar size and attics with dry storage'.
There was also a stable. By comparing the Ferneyhough
drawings of 1823 with two drawings, showing the front and
side of the High House, made by John Buckler in the 1840s,
the extent of the conversion carried out by Henry Jenkinson
can be seen. He had removed the side entrance and replaced
it by a new doorway inserted in the Greengate Street frontage.
Because the level of the ground floor was well above street
level, the new doorway was set back to allow steps within the
building. He had also put in new and larger shop windows
on both frontages, made two ground floor rooms into one
shop and made a new barrel access to the warehouse under the
front window.

The second auction also included five small houses at
the rear of the building. These may have been the two

cottages mentioned in the 1792 sale plus a new brick built
row adjoining the High House and facing St Mary's Gate. This
was later converted to house a curiosity shop. The 1823
drawings show a wall with a door into the yard on this site
but, by the 1840s, houses have been built there, almost
certainly during Henry Jenkinson's work in 1826/7.

All the property above was occupied at the time of the
second auction. Henry Jenkinson and the workmen he employed
must have worked very quickly after the Ferneyhoughs moved
out. The new shop and its living accomodation was occupied
by Richard Ward, a saddler. He must have moved into this
part of the High House late in 1826 and probably stayed until
the summer of 1827, when he moved to the future number 52
Greengate Street. Ward had been born in Penkridge and
apprenticed to Richard Williams, a Stafford saddler. When
Williams died in 1824, Ward had taken over his former master's
business.

Lot 2 was described in the earlier sale notice as 'a
messuage and shop with a stable, capable of being enlarged
to any extent'. In the second sale notice this has become
'two houses and shops occupied by Mr Henry Jenkinson, who
carries on a business there as a dealer in glass and
perfumery'. The existence of the projecting porch and
steps made it difficult to put large shop windows in the
central part of the building. In 1827, it is probable that
only one shop existed in the south/centre part of the High
House and that Henry Jenkinson had simply inserted a new
door and windows into the southern end of the building to
match those he had inserted at the north end. He and his
family occupied the whole of the main dwelling. At the same
time, he clearly intended to create a third shop in the
central part of the property.

Neither lot was sold in the auction in March 1827.
Henry Jenkinson and his family continued to occupy the main
dwelling with the shop he had created at the southern end of
the building. Richard Ward probably continued to occupy
the smaller dwelling and its corner shop until the summer
of 1827, when he moved to the future number 52 Greengate
Street and a new tenant, John Marson, took over the premises.

John Marson, grocer tea dealer and coffee roaster opened his shop there on 15 September 1827.

Work on the conversion of the building came to a halt in 1827, although a difficult-to-interpret notice in The Staffordshire Advertiser in March 1828 may indicate that internal changes were still being made at that time. The advertisement was inserted by Henry Jenkinson and gave notice of a sale of his surplus furniture because he was 'removing to the next house, being connected with his shop'.

Developments in the next few years have to be pieced together mainly from entries in the town chamberlains' accounts recording annual payments for the porch and steps at the High House and from a few surviving land tax assessments. These seem to show that in 1831/2 Henry Jenkinson sold the freehold of the corner shop to John Marson and used the money to complete the conversion of the High House by removing the porch and steps and creating a third shop with a new door and windows in the central part of the building. This was a lock-up with no living accomodation. In December 1833 it was let to Caroline Shelton, a dressmaker.

At some time after 1834, Henry Jenkinson let his own shop at the south end of the building to two brothers Walter and Henry Tanner. These grocers, tea dealers and Italian warehousemen already had a shop in Lichfield. Walter moved to Stafford to take charge of the new shop and moved his family into the living accomodation connected to it. Henry Jenkinson moved into a lock-up shop further down Greengate Street but continued to live in part of the High House. In the attic there can still be seen one of his daughter's scribbles, 'Annie Jenkinson - Amy Wray, two very good girls, 1840'. The Jenkinsons were still living in the High House when the 1841 census was taken.

At some time in either 1843 or 1844 Henry Jenkinson sold the freehold of the other two shops to John Marson, who thus became the owner of the whole of the building. Henry Jenkinson moved his family to living accomodation above his lock-up shop. If the figures given in White's

History, Gazeteer and Directory of Staffordshire (1851) are
accurate, Henry Jenkinson paid £1575 (1500 guineas) for
the building and sold it to John Marson for about £2500.
After allowing for the cost of conversion, this was still a
profitable investment. Not everyone in the town approved
of the scheme. Captain Ferneyhough wrote that the High
House's 'venerable appearance had been destroyed by a
person of bad taste.'

The three shops into which the High House had been
converted each has its own story after the conversion. In
1850, when premises in Stafford were given individual numbers,
they became numbers 47,48 and 49 Greengate Street with
John Marson's corner shop being number 49. The following
chapters give brief accounts of each of the three.

The High House
redrawn from
sketches by
John Buckler
dated
July 1845
(right)
and June 1841
(below).

NUMBER FORTY SEVEN

After the Tanner brothers left Stafford at the end of 1843, Charles Cooper, a tailor and draper who had previously had a shop in Eastgate Street, moved into that part of the High House. Like almost all shopkeepers, he lived on the premises and also employed three live-in apprentices to help him manage a busy shop. He stocked inexpensive but fashionable clothes for men and boys and relied heavily on eye-catching advertisements. His clothes had 'Ease, Elegance and Economy'. In May 1849, under the headline 'Save Your Fare to London!', he promised customers a handsome cloth jacket, a summer vest (waistcoat), doeskin trousers, a Paris velvet hat, a gentleman's shirt, a silk neckerchief, a pocket handkerchief, gloves and socks - all for £5.

In March 1852 he set up his own manufacture of shirts, employing out-workers to make up the garments in their own homes. His advertising stressed that he paid fair wages. None of his shirts were made by sempstresses working long hours for low pay like those in Thomas Hood's well known poem 'The Song of the Shirt', published a few years earlier. With the opening of this manufacture and the need to cut out on the premises, he found space in the High House too limited and at the end of 1852 Charles Cooper moved to larger premises in Market Square.

The next tenants of number 47 were Ingram and Holmes, ironmongers and dealers in china and glass. They already had a shop in Rugeley. Francis Holmes, the junior partner, moved to Stafford to manage the new shop in the High House. A few years later the partnership was dissolved. Ingram remained in Rugeley and Francis Holmes retained the Stafford shop. A selection of his advertisements over the next three decades shows what a nineteenth century ironmonger stocked and the services he provided. 'Furnishing and General Ironmonger, Brazier, Tin and Zinc Plate Worker; Locksmith and Bell Hanger'; 'Experienced workmen sent out at the shortest notice to repair locks, stoves, etc'; Hammerless and other loading guns sold, re-stocked and repaired'; 'Maker of Stafford and Challenger cartridges'; Lawnmowers ground and repaired'; 'The

Sheffield saw and tool warehouse, carpenters' and joiners' tools stocked'. In the 1890s Holmes added The Izaak Walton Fishing Tackle Department. About 1890 he also moved out of the living accomodation on the upper floors and soon afterwards these were let to The Swan as extra bedrooms. In 1899 Holmes sold the business to Robert McBean, who carried on business as an ironmonger, gun maker, gas fitter and cycle repairer until 1912.

In 1912 the Stafford Gas Company (in those days the town had its own gasworks) acquired a lease of the premises for their showrooms and offices. In order to provide more space it was decided to remove the chimney stack on that side of the building. It was found that the building's timber framing was quite independent of the stack and that its stability in no way depended on it. When it was removed, it exposed a portion of the outside wall of the adjoining building. This wall showed signs of weathering at some time, indicating that it had been erected before the High House. When the town's gas works closed and gas was supplied on a regional, and later national, basis, this part of the High House became the showroom of the West Midland Gas Board and, later, The British Gas Energy Centre. In 2002, after another re-organisation of the gas industry, the showroom was closed.

The premises are now occupied by Savers.

NUMBER FORTY EIGHT

The first tenant of the lock-up shop created in the central part of the High House was a dressmaker, Caroline Shelton. She had been a live-in assistant to Elizabeth Bott, whose dressmaking business occupied the same premises as her father's tailoring shop. In Aug 1833 Miss Bott had retired and handed over to Caroline Shelton the goodwill of the business, together with all her patterns and an on-going arrangement for new patterns of the latest fashions to be sent from London. Miss Shelton carried on the busines in John Bott's premises until December 1833, when she moved to the High House 'next to Mr Marson, the grocer'.

In the autumn of 1838, Miss Shelton gave up her shop. and in December it was let to Ralph Broadhurst, a hat manufacturer who specialised in beaver-fur covered hats. He promised 'an extensive stock, on terms hitherto unknown in the district'. His stock included ladies' beavers; children's and youths' fancy beavers; a variety of cloth and silk velvet caps; double cover gentlemen's beavers with short naps, which were light, elastic, waterproof and guaranteed to retain their shape and colour; travelling and other caps. At the beginning of 1841 Ralph bought the business and stock of William Churton, a hatter in Market Square who had recently died. At the time of the 1841 census, he was living in Market Square while continuing his business from the lock-up shop in the High House. His business declined as fashions in hats changed and in 1843 he gave up the High House shop and concentrated his business in the Market Square premises.

About the same time, Henry Jenkinson decided to sell the future numbers 47 and 48 to John Marson. Marson then advertised the lock-up shop to let but without success. Shortly afterwards, Jenkinson moved his family out of his living accomodation in the High House and John Marson was able to re-advertise as 'a house and shop to let' in November 1844. The premises were taken by George Barber, a butcher who already had shops in Gaolgate Street and Gaol Square. Barber lived in part of the High House until 1849/50 when he closed his shop and moved out.

The next tenant was Charles Walker, draper, milliner and
dealer in baby linen. About 1856 he sold the business to
Joseph Marsh. Marsh's advertisements list some of the things
on sale in the shop - trimmed bonnets, widows' bonnets and caps,
crinolines, skirts, shawls, mantles, falls, collars, sunshades,
and cloths such as alpacas, coburgs, baratheas and paramattas.
His advertisements always refer to his premises being in The
Old House. The name High House seems to have fallen into
disuse until it was revived by John Marson in the second
half of the nineteenth century.

Joseph Marsh stayed until about 1868. After that Jane
Read, a fancy milliner and hosier, was there from 1868 to 1872
and then George Henry Rice, a draper. He moved in after the
lease of his Market Square shop expired and was not renewed,
and stayed until about 1878.

After these short lived and not very memorable tenancies,
the premises were let to Pollock & Cowley, tailors and drapers.
Pollock withdrew from the partnership after a few years,
leaving John Cowley to carry on alone as Cowley & Co. Cowley,
who came from the Isle of Man, built up a considerable trade
with English men in the colonies. He kept customers measure-
ments on file and supplied clothes to order for those living
in the remote parts of South Africa, Canada and Australia. In
the 1880s, he employed ten men, some as shop assistants and
others as outworkers making up garments.

One of the assistants, who started work as a shop boy
at the age of 12 in 1904, later recalled that when he started
to work for Mr Cowley the family - Mr and Mrs Cowley and
their two sons - all worked in the shop and lived in the High
House. He was expected to do jobs about the house as well as
in the shop. He was also expected to deliver parcels of clothes
in his own time, but was allowed to keep any tips he might get.
The shop opened at 8.00 a.m. and stayed open until Mottram's
shop, a competitor, opposite closed. On Fridays and Saturdays
this would often be after 10.00 p.m. In 1938 John Cowley sold
the business to W.E.Steventon and in the 1950s it became
Steventon and Keene.

By the 1930s shopkeepers no longer lived above their
shops. In 1936 some of the space above number 48 became the

24

Stafford Foot Clinic, managed by Mrs Gordon. In order to
provide access to the clinic between numbers 48 and 49, the
chimney stack on that side of the building was cut through
on the ground floor. By the 1950s the premises were
occupied by G.B.Cartwright, chiropodist. In the 1950s one
of the upper rooms was also Elizabeth Inston's ladies'
hairdressing salon. Other rooms became extra bedrooms
attached to The Swan.

In the 1960s some of these bedrooms were used as
accomodation for students of Stafford College. This led
to the first reported haunting of the High House. In January
1964 the students were in the habit of holding seances in
their rooms to forecast the results of matches for their
football pools. After one of these sessions, "Adge" Stani-
forth reported seeing a 'wavy white shape that looked rather
like an arm', and Brian Buxton heard knocking on the door of
his room, although no one was there. Neither student was
particularly alarmed but the incident was headlined in The
Newsletter. Since the restoration of the building there have
been other reports of ghostly figures on the upper floors.

About 1970 Sportsco , selling euipment and clothing for
all kinds of sports and games, moved into the shop previously
occupied by Steventon & Keene. By that time concern was being
expressed about the state of the building and the need for
urgent maintainance. In 1975 the Borough Council commissioned
a report from F.W.Charles, an architect specialising in the
restoration of timber-framed buildings. The building was
acquired from the owners and a ten year programme of restoration begun. This included the removal of the shop at number
48 and its replacement by a replica of the original porch and
steps. Sportsco moved from number 48 to number 49 in 1982.

The restoration and opening of the High House to the
public is described in more detail in the next chapter.

NUMBER FORTY NINE

John Marson, a grocer, tea dealer and coffee roaster, opened his corner shop in the High House on 15 September 1827. For three years previously he had been in London, trading in tea and attending the tea auctions of the East India Company, which had a monopoly of the import of tea. His new shop stocked 'Souchong, Pekoe, Padrae, Tetsong Hyson, Gunpowder, Young Hyson, Bloom and Twankay Teas of the finest possible flavour and quality'. Families and inns ordering a chest of tea could have it cleared direct from

The High House in 1859 from a print by R & W Wright

the East India Company warehouse.

In 1831/2 John Marson bought the freehold of his shop and about 1843 the freehold of the rest of the High House. In May 1854 he made considerable alterations to his property, particularly to his own corner shop. These can be seen by comparing the Buckler drawings of the 1840s with a print of 'Old Houses in Greengate Street' published by R. & W. Wright in 1859. The relevant part of the print is reproduced on the previous page.

The principal changes made were the lowering of the ground floor level, almost to the level of the street, in the corner shop, and probably in the other shops as well, and the insertion of a corner doorway into number 49. To do this part of the main corner post of the house had to be cut away. This weakened the building and caused later structural damage. A new front window with three tall plate glass panes was put into the corner shop. The windows of the other two shops were different and were probably not changed.

John had apprenticed his sons James and William to grocers in large towns to learn the trade and in 1863 they took over the business. James, the elder brother, died in 1876 and William then became the sole proprietor of number 49. Many years later, he wrote, 'As soon as I was established in my position I set to work to improve everything. I went for the first class family trade. I started going round for orders in Stafford. I soon made the old shop look a bit like a London one and stocked goods that were almost unknown - Crystallised Fruits, Turtle, Sardines, Sauces of all kinds, Bottled Fruits, and Fancy Carton Boxes of Plums! He even imported groceries from China and Japan.

A few years later, he decided to modernise the fronts of all three shops. A newspaper cutting now in the William Salt Library and dated March 1885 reported, ' The new windows have bold, solid frames, which give an appearance of stability to the old structure, and by the addition of tiles, a warmth of tone has been imparted which is a great gain. The upper part of the windows of Mr W.A.Marson's shop have been broken up by the introduction of transoms and mullions, thus diminishing their apparent height and giving the opportunity for the introduction of stained glass by Mr Swaine Bourne of Birmingham. The subjects in the glass of Mr Marson's shop are The Borough Arms (in the fanlight over the entrance), the Marson family crest and arms in the central window with cartoons of tea and coffee plants in flower on either side. In the window of Mr Cowley's shop, his trade is represented by fifteenth century costumes , weaving, spinning and cutting out garments and a sheep in the fanlight over the door. Mr Holmes has in his window cartoons representing gridirons, bells, swords, guns and workers at an anvil. Over the door is the crest of the ancient family of Holmes.

'The front of the building has been further enriched by carvings. The gable over Mr Holmes' door has a medallion of Izaak Walton, the gable over Mr Cowley's door has the head of a cavalier, and in the cove over Mr Cowley's shop is carved a British Lion with its mouth open for purposes

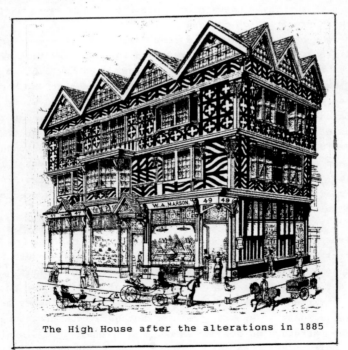

The High House after the alterations in 1885

of gas ventilation.

'The woodwork of the various shops has been painted in dark oak, while the coves in cornices are a cream colour, on which will appear the various names of the occupiers in quaint letters. The whole of the work has been carried out under the supervision of the architect, Mr George Wormald.'

William Marson, in addition to being a grocer, was agent for a Liverpool shipping line and published an account of his own travels to promote this side of his business. He was also a keen photographer and many of his early photographs of the places he visited are now in the William Salt Library. He was a church organist and a lay preacher. He was a long-serving member of the town council and was chosen as mayor in 1905.

About 1890 he opened an Old Curiosity Shop in St Mary's Gate, at the rear of the High House. There he sold antique furniture, curios, clocks, mirrors, barometers, musical instruments, china, plate, etc. About 1910 the Curiosity Shop closed and was replaced by Tea Rooms. William Marson lived in the High House until about 1890 when he moved to a house on Newport Road. In 1908 he sold his business and the High House to R.J.Young, who continued to trade as W.A. Marson & Co until the 1940s.

The High House in the 1950s.

R.J.Young died in 1946, leaving the High House to his daughter, Mrs W.Dean. By 1954 , number 49 was let to Heath and Heather, selling herbal remedies, pot pourri, soap, lavender, pomanders and similar items. In the 1960s it became Harry Fenton, men's wear.

By 1972 the condition of the building was causing concern. The conversion into shops and removal of part of the main corner post in the nineteenth century had weakened the structure. In places damp penetration was causing timbers to rot. The Borough Council, anxious to preserve the building, commissioned a report from F.W.Charles, an architect specialising in timber-framed buildings. His report showed that restoration was possible and the Council then began negotiations to acquire the building. These were successfully concluded in 1976.

The Council then embarked on a ten year programme of restoration. Damaged timber was replaced and the building restored as nearly as possible to its original form. On the ground floor, the shops at numbers 47 and 49 were retained, but that at 48 was removed to allow the construction of a replica of the original entrance porch and steps. Sportsco, moved from 48 to the vacant shop at 49 in 1982 and remained until 1990/1, when they moved to larger premises. From 1992 to 2006 number 49 was the Cancer Research Campaign's charity shop. It is now Natural Heath: herbs and acupuncture.

The restoration of the High House was completed in 1986 and in June of that year it was opened to the public as a museum and Tourist Information Centre. In 2000 the Tourist Information Centre moved to Market Street, allowing more space for displays and a souvenir shop in the High House. Since 1986, rooms in the house have gradually been furnished in period styles and displays mounted to show different periods in the history of the building. 'The Friends of the High House' was formed to support this work and encourage local people to take an active interest in the project. An extensive educational programme for young people has also been inaugurated.

NUMBERS FIFTY, FIFTY ONE and FIFTY TWO

A narrow alley, St Mary's Gate, lies between the High
House and numbers 50-52. Until the mid-twentieth century the
building on the corner opposite the High House was older than
the High House itself. This timber-framed building, called
the Talbot, had been built in the early sixteenth century
with three gables facing the street. At the beginning of the
eighteenth century additional space was created by turning the
gables into attics and inserting small windows into the gable
ends, as can be seen in the engraving below.

Numbers 50-52 engraved from a
drawing by J.R.Ferneyhough, 1823

Robert Sutton was appointed the first rector of St Mary's
church in 1572. When he died in 1588, he left his whole
estate to the Corporation for charitable purposes. Each year
four poor scholars at the Grammar School were to be given one
noble (26s 8d) each; the rents from the rest of his property
were to be distributed to the poor or used for repairs to the
church and school. Among his property was the Talbot, which he
had leased to John Collins at an annual rent of £10 until
Sutton died and then a reduced rent of £5. Collins was the
town bailiff in 1603 and died in June 1605. His widow paid
the town chamberlains threepence in 1606, because the posts
and sign of the Talbot encroached on the street. In 1607 she

married John Wakering and continued to occupy The Talbot, although Sutton's lease had expired when John Collins died, and the Corporation was trying to evict her. John Wakering died in December 1614. Anne Wakering, widow, described as an innkeeper or keeper of a common alehouse, was still at The Talbot in 1615. She was evicted soon afterwards. The new licensee has not been identified. Soon afterwards The Talbot ceased to be an inn and the name was not used.

In 1690 the Talbot was leased to widow Ellen Mott, who paid £10 for her lease plus an annual rent of £5 which was used to pay the four scholars. The lease, which was for her life and the lives of John and Thomas Mott, was probably a renewal of an earlier lease to her husband. The lease ended in 1708.

The property was then described as 'a large old house standing in Greengate Street at the corner of a lane leading to the church, containing a great quantity of building, very ruinous and out of repair'. The Corporation had no money for repairs and put the property up for sale to the highest bidder. It was sold to James Eaton, who bid £100 for it and agreed to pay an annual sum of £5-6-8 to the Corporation for the benefit of 'Sutton's nobles'. The £100 was put towards the purchase of a house in Greengate Street for the use of the rector of St Mary's.

In 1736 it was reported that 'James Eaton has since 1708 laid out great sums in repairing the house and has converted it into several tenements, now bringing in a sum of £20 a year'. Eaton was a joiner or carpenter and had obviously used his skills to restore the building. He had made himself a house on the corner of St Mary's Gate and converted the rest of the property into three small apartments which he let to Widow Tanner, Widow Adams and Peter Hatton.

About 1760, James Eaton junior, old James's son, inherited the property. He did not live there but let the corner house, where his father had lived, to Thomas Westbrook, who opened a cutler's shop there. In 1787 he sold the whole property to the unusually named Sturmee Maulin, who continued to let the shop to Thomas Westbrook and the rest of the house to three elderly tenants.

Thomas Westbrook died at the beginning of 1807. The new tenant was Job Jameson, a hairdresser and perfumier. His American descendants claimed that Job had owned the High House, but this is untrue. Job died in 1826. Sturmee Maulin had died a few years earlier in 1819 and the property passed to Richard Beech.

32

In 1826/7 Richard Beech rebuilt the front and south side
of the premises. His new brick front, with new new windows,
was little more than a shell, within which most of the old sixteenth century building remained. At the same time, internal
alterations were made to convert the premises into three small
shops, each with its own living accomodation. In 1850, when
numbers were allocated to premises in Greengate Street, these
became numbers 50, 51 and 52.

Their separate histories after 1826 are recounted below.

The rent charge of four nobles has remained payable,
although it is no longer paid to four poor scholars but used
for more general educational purposes.

NUMBER FIFTY

The first tenant of the rebuilt number 50 was probably
Mr Daines, who gave up the shop when Richard Cope became the
tenant in October 1836. Cope's shop sold glass, china and
cutlery, although his main business was making and selling covers
for wagons and ricks. He also sold heavy duty bags, nets and
rope. He was living above the shop at the time of the census
in June 1841 and his name can be seen above the shop in the
Buckler drawing reproduced on page 20. However, he had closed
the shop and moved out before the end of 1841.

The new tenant was William Wynne, a boot and shoe
manufacturer, the Wynne family had been making shoes in
Stafford since the beginning of the nineteenth century.
William Wynne, born in 1810, had set up his own business at
Snow Hill in 1832 and by the late 1830s had moved to 51
Greengate Street, where he opened a retail shop as an
addition to his business. He prospered. In the 1840s he
was employing 80 or more outworkers to make up shoes from
leather cut out in a room at the back of his shop. Space was

limited and when 'more commodious' premises became vacant
at number 50 at the end of 1841 he moved into them. This
property had the advantage of a rear entrance from St Mary's
Gate, making it easier for outworkers to come and go. Wynne
had been a tenant at number 51 but seems to have bought 50.
In December 1846 The Staffordshire Advertiser reported that
he had just put in 'a handsome new shop front'.

Number 50, showing the
handsome shop front put in
in 1846. From an engraving
by R. and W. Wright in 1859.

     In the 1850s the introduction of sewing machines for
making the uppers of shoes threatened the livelihoods of
outworkers. They attempted to ban the use of the machines.
In 1855, it was probably William Wynne who provoked a strike
by asking his outworkers to make up boots using uppers that
had been machine sewn in another town. Eventually, the outworkers had to accept the new machines and manufacturers had
to build factories to house them. Wynne had no space for a
factory and did not make the transition to a factory based
manufacturer. By 1865 his shop was selling boots and shoes

made by other manufacturers and bespoke boots made by his two remaining employees.

The following advertisement shows how his shop developed a speciality in boots. 'William Wynne, family bootmaker. Depot for K and City K scout boots; cloth and leather gaiters; repairs neatly executed; slippers carefully made up; customers living at a distance waited on by appointment. Hunting, grooms, fishing and shooting boots to order by first class workmen. Polished boot trees made to order.'

William Wynne married twice, his second wife being 14 years younger than he was. At the time of the 1881 census he was 71, his wife Lucy 57 and their daughter, also Lucy, 12. After he died, his widow and eldest son William Wyatt Wynne carried on the business, living above the shop until about 1900. After they moved out, the upper floor was let to Lea, Sons & Co, electrical engineers and manufacturers, whose works were in Shrewsbury but who maintained an agent and office in Stafford until 1919.

In 1901 William Wyatt Wynne put in new plate glass windows facing Greengate Street and St Mary's Gate with a curved widow in the corner. At the same time, he refitted the interior and extended the range of ladies' and gentlemen's shoes stocked. He retired in 1908 and his half-sister Lucy took over the management of the shop.

In 1915 Brookfield's, who already occupied numbers 51 and 52, bought number 50. Brookfield's had been a gentlemen's outfitters and now extended their business into ladies' fashions. Number 50 was refitted to provide a ladies' shoe department at the front of the shop and a ladies' clothes department further back, with an entrance from St Mary's Gate.

The later history of the whole of the premises numbered 50 to 52 is recounted after the earlier history of numbers 51 and 52.

NUMBER FIFTY ONE

This was the middle one of three shops created when the building was given a new front in the 1820s. After rebuilding, the first tenant was almost certainly Joseph Elley, a small scale shoe manufacturer. He also opened a retail shop at number 51. He vacated the premises in the late 1830s. They were then let to another shoe manufacturer,William Wynne. Wynne stayed until the end of 1841, when he took over the larger number 50 and moved his business and shop there.

Johm Bagnall moved into number 51 in March 1842. The shop was re-fitted to sell an assortment of groceries,teas, coffee and spices. John died in 1863 and his widow, Sarah, carried on until February 1864 when ill health forced her to give up the shop and move away.

The next tenant was Helen Deacock, a milliner from London who had moved to Stafford some years earlier and had had a shop next to The Swan. She advertised as 'Mode-de-Paris' and made twice yearly visits to both London and Paris to choose stock for her spring and autumn collections, leaving her live-in assistant Jane Scheegaus in charge. The shop closed in July 1871 when Helen Deacock moved to Manchester.

The premises were taken over by Lovatt & Woodall, milliners and mantle makers, who already had a shop at 55 Greengate Street. Their second shop at number 51 opened in September 1871. It remained open for three years before being sold to Mary and Jane Harrold, milliners and dressmakers in 1874. They stayed until early 1881, when Thomas Jenkins, a draper who already had a shop elsewhere, moved in. He remained until late 1884.

From 1885 to 1890 the premises were occupied by John Jervis,stationer, newsagent, and local agent for the British & Foreign Bible Society. Jervis, born at Tixall in 1856, had lost an arm in an accident while he was still a youth. He had begun work with The Staffordshire Advertiser but in 1885 left the newspaper to start his own business. He was the local correspondent of several midland papers, a lay preacher and secretary of the Stafford Rechabites. In 1890 he moved to a larger shop at 5 Greengate Street.

After this succession of short-stay shops, William
Wright opened a successful drapery shop in the premises and
remained there for the the next twenty years. He moved out
in 1910.   In that year, Brookfield's, on the opposite side
of the street, closed and their chief buyer, trading under
the name Brookfield's, opened a new shop at numbers 51 and
52.   The history of this shop is related after the brief
history of number 52 that follows.

NUMBER FIFTY TWO
     This was the third and most northerly of the three
shops created when the building was altered in the late
1820s.   Unlike the other two, it not only had a new brick
front that was plastered over, but also had its roof raised
to give an extra storey and a bay window, overlooking the
street, added to the living quarters on the first floor.
     Richard Ward, a saddler and harness maker, who had
briefly occupied a shop in the High House, opened a shop
here in the summer of 1827.   In February 1849 he took into
partnership his nephew Richard Boyden, who had several years
experience working for a London saddler. He then handed
over his share of the business to his son Richard junior.
At the time of the 1851 census, Richard junior was living
on the premises with his younger brother Thomas, who was
learning the trade, four men and a 15 year old apprentice.
Richard junior left the business in the 1850s and Richard
Boyden moved into the living quarters and carried on the
business until 1889.   Directories of the town suggest that
Richard Ward may have returned as a partner in the 1860s
and that the shop traded as Ward and Boyden from about 1866
to 1880.
     Richard Boyden sold the business to Henry Glaze in 1889.
Glaze did not live on the premises and let the upper floors
to his senior assistant Edward Upton. In 1910 the business
closed and the premises, together with number 51, were
taken over and refitted as a gentlemen's outfitter, trading
as Brookfield's.

Brookfield's in 1910

In 1909 Arthur Brookfield retired and closed his department store on the eastern side of Greengate Street. Heads of department in the store were encouraged to set up in business for themselves, taking with them the goodwill of their old department. C.H.Smith, chief buyer in the men's outfitting department, and his assistant H.S.Tomkinson acquired numbers 51 and 52 Greengate Street, which they refitted as a gentlemen's outfitter. They were allowed to retain the name Brookfields. They bought the entire stock of their old department and in February 1910 opened their new shop with a grand sale of oddments and last season's lines. Surplus space on the upper floor was let to Frederick Pickering, dentist and maker of artificial teeth, and in the 1930s to J.W.Peach, chiropodist. He stayed until 1962.

The shop remained a gentlemen's outfitter until 1919 when the business expanded into number 50 and added ladies' shoe and clothes departments. At the same time other parts of the shop were refitted. In the 1930s a fictitious black and white pattern was painted on the plaster at the front of the shop to suggest that this was a timber framed building. New ground floor display windows were put in after the 1939-45 War .

STAFFORDS

New Department Store

for

LADIES' - MEN'S - CHILDREN'S
FASHIONS AND DRESS FABRICS

RENDEZVOUS IN THE STUDIO
COFFEE LOUNGE

BRATT & DYKE

GREENGATE — STAFFORD 52301

The new Bratt & Dyke
Department Store, 1965

In 1930 Eric and Sydney Smith took over the shop from their father. When they retired in 1964, they sold the property to Bratt & Dyke, a family firm founded in 1890. The new owners demolished the old building, and in its place built a 4 storey department store with 3 showroom floors and a coffee shop. The top floor was used as offices and for staff facilities. The first, ground-floor phase of the new store opened in November 1966 and the rest early the following year. The store closed in the early 1970s and the premises were taken over by Cantor's furniture store, which occupied the premises until 1981.

The building was then altered extensively, with new projecting first floor windows, a new ground floor frontage, and internal division into two units. The corner unit, approximately the site of 50 and 51, became MacDonald's Golden Arches Restaurant, and the unit on the site of 52 became a branch of the Yorkshire Bank

NUMBER FIFTY THREE

Number 53 based on a
drawing by J.R.Ferneyhough
in 1823.

The tall, three storey house seen in the 1823 drawing
probably dated from the first half of the eighteenth century.
The history of the building at that period is uncertain.
Probably, it was the home of William Godwin as early as 1735
and, later, of his son George, a shoe manufacturer. In 1787
George sold the property to Charles Yates, a glover. Yates
covered the brick front with plaster and added a ground floor
bay window where he could display his gloves. He lived
there until 1820 but in 1812   sublet part of the premises
to Sarah Worsey, a dressmaker. When Yates moved out in 1820,
Sarah bought the property and made her home there. Her
daughter Anne joined her mother in the dressmaking business
and carried it on after her mother died.

In July 1826 Sarah Worsey let part of the property to
William Batty a shoe manufacturer with a warehouse and count-
ing house in St Mary's Lane. He opened a retail shoe warehouse at number 53. This was not a success and it closed in
1828. The premises were then let to Henry Brindley, a saddler
and harness maker with extensive London experience, who had
come to Stafford and opened a shop in Eastgate Street a few
months earlier. Brindley stayed only until the end of 1829,
when he moved to number 54 Greengate Street.

In April 1830 John Earp, a tailor who had lived in
London for several years and worked in fashionable tailors'
shops in the West End, opened a shop in the premises vacated
by Henry Brindley. His London connections attracted those
who desired garments cut according to the latest fashions
and John Earp made sure that customers knew that his links
with the London fashion trade were maintained. His
visits to London 'to select a most elegant and fashionable
assortment of patterns' were advertised in The Staffordshire
Advertiser. As well as gentlemen's clothes, the shop supplied
ladies' riding habits and servants' liveries. At the end of
1831 John Earp became seriously ill. He died in January 1832
leaving his widow, Elizabeth, to carry on the business with
'the help of a London trained foreman'. Earp's posthumous son
was born the following summer and in September his widow was
forced to transfer the business to smaller and cheaper
premises near the gates at the east end of St Mary's churchyard.

Anne Worsey then decided to sell the vacant premises.
They were bought by James Marson, who came from a family of
yeomen who had lived at Leigh for several generations before
moving to Acton Trussell. When he opened his new shop in
December 1832, he described himself as 'a wholesale and retail
druggist and operative chemist'. He stocked 'genuine drugs
and chemicals; patent medicines; perfumery; oils; colours;
fish sauces; spices; London garden seeds; horse and cattle
medicines; wax, composition, Kensington and cocoa fibre
candles; etc.' There was a separate counter for poisons.
For the next 120 years number 53 was to remain a chemist's
shop.

James Marson took an active part in local government in
the 1830s and was offered the post of being the first mayor
after the reforms of The Municipal Corporations Act (1835).
He declined. Before 1859 he had replaced his old shop with
the three storey, plain, brick building which is still there
today. He had a large family of six daughters and eight
sons. His fourth son William became a partner in the shop
and carried on the business after his father died in 1870.
In the 1880s William moved out of the living accomodation

41

above the shop and bought a house in Eastgate Street. He was
elected onto the town council in 1894 and was chosen as
mayor in 1906/6. His favourite sport was shooting and he
was also a keen fisherman. In February 1917 he had a serious
heart attack while walking in Castle Fields with his brother.
He recovered slowly but died in 1918.

He had never married and after his death the shop was
sold to Henry and John Eymer, the sons of John Eymer, senior,
a pattern cutter at Bostock's shoe factory. Both brothers
were qualified pharmacists and John was also an optician.
They continued to trade as Marson & Son although Eymer Bros
was often added in brackets. They had a particular interest
in photography and in the 1920s their shop was the local
depot for Kodak films and cameras. They even re-christened
their premises Camera House, but the name was little used
by the public and was soon dropped. Henry was a prominent
member of the Congregational Church in the town . He was also
a councillor and was chosen as mayor in 1924.

When the Eymers retired in 1953, Elkes, the Uttoxeter
confectionery company, opened a bakery, café and restaurant
at number 53. By 1960 the premises were occupied by Rosewall
Ltd, selling wallpaper and decorators' materials. In the late
1970s The Anglia Building Society put in a new ground floor
frontage and opened a branch there. After the society
amalgamated with The Nationwide Building Society in 1987,
there was a duplication of branches in the town and the
branch at 53 Greengate Street was closed.

The building was then refitted as a shop and became
Trawlers Fish Restaurant and Take-away from about 1990 to
1997. It is now Thornton's chocolate and confectionery
shop.

NUMBER FIFTY FOUR

Numbers 54 and 55 based on a
drawing by J.R.Ferneyhough
in 1823.

The earliest drawing of this house, made in 1823, shows
a building with a steep gable facing Greengate Street and
marked with an improbable pattern of black and white, which
must be painted on plaster rather than showing genuine timber
framing. Shop windows had been added to the ground floor.

In 1731 the house was owned by Richard Mountford and
let to Thomas Spencer and, later, to John Washbrook. About 1748
Mountford sold the house to widow Smith, who made her home
there until 1757. It was then occupied by John Stevenson.
About 1780 he sold the building to Charles Clarke. Clarke
let it to the surgeon Richard Adams until 1788/9 and then to
Robert Hill, a clock and watch maker and repairer. It was
probably at this time that shop windows were built into the
ground floor of what had been a house.   In 1797 the property was bought by Peter Brown, a hatter and feltmaker,
living in the adjoining shop (number 55). Brown allowed
Robert Hill to go on living above his shop until he died in
1804. Hill's widow then carried on for another six years.

The next tenant was Samuel Braddock. He had taken over
a grocery and tea shop in Market Square when Thomas Hammersley
became bankrupt in 1807. By 1811 Hammersley's creditors had
been paid off and he moved back into his shop. Braddock
moved to number 54, where he opened his own grocery and tea
shop. He remained there until March 1815.

In April 1815 John Rogers, a bookseller and stationer,
refitted the ground floor premises and opened a shop there.
Besides books and stationery, Rogers advertised that he could

43

procure magazines and bind books. He also sold hanging paper
(wallpaper) in the most modern patterns; ladies fancy articles
painted on velvet; Mason's Belle-isle Convent soap (as used
by the Royal Family) with transparent delicacy and ethereal
whiteness; Parisian tooth powder; La Poudre sans Pareille to
remove superfluous hair from face, neck and arms; and Tinctura
Parmanens to change grey hair to brown. In 1820 he bought a
hand press and began printing letterheads, notices and leaf-
lets.   At the end of 1829 he moved into larger premises
at number 56.

The next tenant was a saddler and harness maker, Henry
Brindley, who had previously occupied a shop lower down
Greengate Street. He stayed until July 1831, when he sold
his business to a young saddler William Shaw. Shaw was also
appointed the local agent for Cox's Birmingham glassworks
and his wife looked after a display of cut and plain glass-
ware in the shop. The display expanded and became a second
business within the saddlery shop, selling glass, china and
earthenware with stock that included papier maché items,
tea urns and candlesticks.   If a customer broke any article
bought in the shop, Shaw guaranteed to match it at short
notice.   In April 1841 his wife died suddenly, leaving him
with young children to look after.   He sold off the stock of
china and glass-ware in May and, shortly afterwards, moved his
saddlery business to a smaller shop in the market place.

John Griffin, a linen draper with a wholesale as well
as a retail business, had had a shop at number 55 for some
30 years.   In 1842 he bought number 54, adjoining his existing
shop, pulled down the old building and rebuilt it as a three
storeyed shop with a bay window on the first floor overlooking
the street and an ornamental gable. He opened his new shop
in April 1843. His building is still there today with altered
ground floor shop windows.   He then separated his retail
and wholesale businesses, making the newly built number 54
his shop and his old premises at 55 the centre for his wholesale business.

John Griffin was well known and well liked in the town.
He was chosen as mayor four times in the 1840s and 1850s. In
the 1860s his wholesale business of John Griffin & Son, shoe

mercers and leather merchants, expanded steadily. After his
death in 1868, his son William turned it into a limited
company with himself as chairman. He did not live on the
premises and moved the limited company into number 54 so
that he could sell the goodwill of the draper's shop with a
lease of number 55. John Griffin & Son remained at number
54 until 1893.

The new owner of the property was Harriet Swanwick, who
opened a shop there selling fish, oysters, game and 'fresh
sausages made daily'. About 1910 the building was altered
to provide a ground floor shop (54) and separate first floor
premises (54A) with its own entrance and ground floor display
window.

Number 54A was first occupied by Agnes Galloway, who
opened The Zetland Café there. In 1911 she moved to Market
Square and the upper floor became Earnest Grocott's Oriental
Café. After that closed in 1914, 54A was occupied by S.
Bagley, Professor Academic International de Coiffure, court
hairdresser and wigmaker. His high class ladies' and gentlemen's salon made a speciality of the new marcel waving.
Families could also be attended in their own homes. By 1920
the salon had closed and the sisters Mabel and Lizzie White
were selling exclusive millinery, blouses and gowns there.
They went bankrupt in 1924. After that the upper rooms
reverted to being a café run by John Hassall, a confectioner
with a shop in St Mary's Place.

Mrs Swanwick carried on her fish shop until 1936 when
she sold the business to MacFisheries, who also acquired 54A.
Although MacFisheries always claimed the address 54 and 54A,
they let the upper floor as a Christian Science reading room
and, later, to John Michaelson, tailor. The Northern Counties
Press Bureau was there in the 1960s.

MacFisheries closed in the late 1970s when Granada TV
took over the premises. They remained until 1985.The premises
were then occupied by The Exchange Travel Agency. In 1990
this became the United Northern Co-operative Society Travel
Agents and is now Co-op Travel Care.

NUMBER FIFTY FIVE

The 1823 drawing of the High House by J.R.Ferneyhough
also shows the future number 55. It has a single steep-sided
gable facing Greengate Street and on the ground floor a bow
window either side of the main doorway. There is a short
flight of steps up to the door. A sketch of the property,
based on Ferneyhough's drawing, is reproduced on page 43.

In the early eighteenth century this was the home of
Abraham Hoskins (or Hodgkins), gentleman. He was mayor in
1708 and again in 1716. In his will, dated February 1732,
he left his house to his eldest son, Abraham junior, with
the proviso that, if Abraham junior had no children, the
house should pass to one of his younger brothers. Abraham
junior was childless and the house descended to another
Abraham, the son of Abraham junior's youngest brother William.
This Abraham Hoskins was a merchant and dealer in Manchester
and therefore let the property to Peter Brown, a hatter and
feltmaker in Stafford.

In 1773 Peter Brown bought the freehold of the building
and altered the ground floor by inserting the bow windows seen
in the 1823 drawing. These gave the house a more fashionable
look and provided a better display for hats. When Peter
Brown died in 1798, his will explained that provision had
already been made for his widow and eldest son. Therefore,
his house and shop were left to his younger son, also named
Peter. Peter junior carried on his father's business until
1811 when he sold the property to John Griffin.

Griffin, who came from Colwich, opened a drapery shop
at number 54 and also ran a wholesale business as a shoe
mercer and leather merchant. In 1842 he bought and rebuilt
the adjoining property (number 54). He then separated his
two businesses, making number into his drapery shop and
number 55 the place from which he ran his wholesale shoe
and leather business. Both businesses became John Griffin
& Son in the early 1860s and, when John Griffin died in
1868, his son William took over.

William moved the wholesale business to number 54 and

turned it into a limited company with himself as chairman.
Number 55 became the retail drapery shop and in 1869 was
sold, together with a lease of the premises, to a partnership of Josiah Lovatt and William Woodall. Lovatt lived
on the premises with the three live-in shop assistants
and a shop boy. By 1881 he no longer lived there and a
housekeeper had been employed to look after the live-in
employees. The shop sold ' a choice selection of the leading novelties in French and English millinery, straw hats,
bonnets and jackets' as well as drapery. 'Costumes for
ladies made to order. Wedding and mourning orders carefully
attended to'.

In September 1874 the partners bought the freehold of
the property and in the following year pulled down the old
building and replaced it with a modern shop with living
accomodation. The new three-storeyed building had prominent
eaves below a low parapet. Its brick front was plastered
over to look like stone. The upper floor windows had ornate
frames with plaster swags. The ground floor shop front has
been altered several times but the rest of the building
remains externally as it was when it was built in 1874.

Josiah Lovatt retired in 1894 and sold his share of
the business to his partner. William Woodall made his son
Alfred manager and traded as Woodall & Son. Alfred moved
into the living accomodation above the shop and, after
William's death in January 1900, his widow made the business
over to him. It remained a family business until it closed
in 1986.

In 1987 Cards & Candy opened a shop there, sharing the
premises with Thornton's confectionery shop until 1998, when
Thornton's moved to number 53. Cards & Candy closed in 2003.
From 2003 until September 2006 the premises were occupied
by Hallmark Cards. In December 2006 Music Zone open a branch
at number 55, but a few weeks later, in January 2007, the
company went into administration and the branch closed. In
June 2007 it was still vacant.

NUMBER FIFTY SIX

A Newsletter report in 1958 claimed that the title deeds
of this property went back to the late sixteenth century.
That could well be the time when this house was constructed.
It is timber-framed, like the High House, and of similar date
but the front has been plastered to make it more weather
proof. New windows were inserted in the late eighteenth or
early nineteenth century but this is still basically a house
of about 1600.

Nothing is known of its history before 1729, when it was
the home of William Rutter. Rutter had been admitted as a
burgess in 1712 and may have been living in the house from
about that date. It was inherited by his son James who
lived there until his death about 1770. In 1772 there is
a reference to a Miss Rutter there- presumably James' daughter - and then a blank until 1788. The property was then
bought by James Cramer, who converted it into a grocer's
and ironmonger's shop, with a pavement door below which was
a chute into the cellars.

Cramer was a local man, born in Stafford in 1760 and
a resident of Greengate Street from 1788 until October 1829,
when he retired to Greenfield Cottage. The cottage grounds
stretched from Garden Street to Wolverhampton Road. He died
there in 1843 and his family continued to live there until
about 1880. The cottage was then sold and Cramer Street
laid out over its grounds. Greenfield Cottage still stands
at the far end of the street.

When Cramer retired, the premises were bought by John
Rogers,a bookseller, stationer and printer, who moved from
a smaller shop at 54 Greengate Street. Rogers had the
largest lending library in the town with over 1,000 volumes in the early 1830s. He was active in local town affairs,
being a councillor for many years and mayor in 1833 and 1841.
In the early 1840s he sold his business to the brothers
Ralph and Walter Wright and retired to Leamington, where he
died in 1858. He left £500 to the Stafford Charity Trustees,
the interest to be used to apprentice three poor children
each year.

R. and W. Wright, as well as being stationers and printers, sold music and musical instruments. In 1849 they advertised flutes, violins and accordions for sale. In 1850 they
had a stock of well seasoned pianos,'powerful with brilliant
tones, selected from the best makers' and also had for sale
'pianos home from hire' at reduced prices. They continued
Rogers' lending library and extended it by establishing a
branch of the London Circulating Library at the shop. In
1847 they printed a catalogue of all the books available on
loan and circulated it to all subscribers. In 1849 they
published four engraved views of St Mary's 'by a well known
artist' at ten shillings a set and in 1859 an engraving of
'The Old Houses in Greengate Street', reproduced on pages
26 and 33.

In an 1886 advertisement they described their business
as, 'Printers, booksellers, book binders, stationers and
music sellers, dealers in piano fortes, harmoniums and
American organs. A large assortment of leather goods, photo-
graph albums and views of Stafford and its vicinity are
always for sale'.

Neither brother was married at the time of the 1851
census and they had no close relatives to whom the business
could be passed. When Ralph retired in the early 1890s, an
employee, S.Roberts, was made a partner. Roberts died in 1896.
W. Wright sold the business to J.A.Wright, who had had his
own business in Gaolgate Street and seems to have not been
a relation, and Henry Charrington, a long serving employee.

Charrington, born in 1860, was the son of a Lichfield
chemist. After serving an apprenticeship with F.W.Meacham,
a Lichfield booksellers and printer, he had joined R. & W.
Wright in 1878. He was a keen motorist and is said to
have owned the first motor car in the town to be registered
under The Motor Car Act (1903). When J.A.Wright died,
Charrington carried on the business alone until 1905,
retaining the name Wright & Charington.

In 1905 W.H. Smith & Son, whose business up to that
time had been organising the daily distribution of newspapers and magazines to newsagents all over the country,

and also selling newspapers and magazines from railway
bookstalls, had decided to branch out into owning shops
where newspapers and books could be sold and local printing carried on. They looked for suitable shops to take
over. They had to be in large towns and in prime trading
positions. Henry Charington was persuaded to retire and
sell number 56 and the goodwill of his business. The shop
was carried on with little change. The upstairs rooms,
reached by a separate entrance, were used as a base from
which newspapers and magazines were distributed to local
newsagents. The company also began publishing its own
Greengate Series of local postcards.

In 1909, when Brookfield's closed, a larger and more
modern shop became available on the opposite site of
Greengate Street. In 1910 W.H.Smith & Son moved their
business, including the printing presses taken over from
Wright & Charington, into number 3 Greengate Street. About
the same time Boots the Chemist bought the Market Square
premises of James Elliott & Co, tailors and outfitters.
Elliott & Co moved into number 56.

In 1920 James Elliott was preparing to retire and had
already appointed his only son Robert as manager in prep-
aration for him taking over the business. In August 1920
Robert became ill, caught pneumonia and died. In 1922
James Elliott sold his business to a newly formed company
Elliott, Stephens & Co, which retained his name although he
no longer had any active involvement in the business. The
new company's advertisements for ladies' costumes, costume
lengths, gentlemen's suits and overcoats, boys clothing,
sports clothes, etc., all give number 56 the name Greengate
House. The company remained there until 1932.

The premises were sold to R.J.Young, trading as
Jenkinson's Ltd. He completely refitted the whole of the
premises and a youthful Walter Dean officially opened the
new restaurant, Brunch Bar and confectionery shop there.
The lay-out was planned to complement Jenkinson's other
shop at number 58. When R.J.Young died in 1946, number
56 was inherited by his daughter, Mrs Walter Dean

A major refurbishment took place in May 1958. This

JENKINSON'S CAFE

(R.J. YOUNG, Proprietor)

All Confectionery guaranteed absolutely
pure and made on the premises

Bride Cakes a
speciality
Wedding parties
catered for

Telephone
30

A
PLACE
TO
MEET
A FRIEND

GREENGATE STREET, STAFFORD

retained the confectionery shop and restaurant with waitress
service, now named The Beefeater, but extended the self-service Brunch Bar by taking in a dining room and the existing
kitchen. New self-service display cabinets were installed
and the kitchen moved upstairs. Further alterations were
made in November 1964 when The Beefeater was given a new
entrance and more space for dancing. Besides morning coffee,
afternoon tea and lunches, it stayed open on Thursday and
Friday evenings until 10.30 for music and dancing to the
Norman Green Trio. Every Saturday there was a dinner dance
until midnight. The premises closed in 1982

They were still vacant in 1983 when a serious fire at 20
Greengate Street left Curry's in urgent need of new premises.
Number 56 was quickly fitted out and Curry's moved in and
stayed until early in 2001, when they moved to larger premises
on the new Madford development.

When Curry's moved out, the shop was again refitted for
Clinton Cards, a company founded by Don Lewin at Epping in
1968 and expanding rapidly with branches over the whole of
the country selling cards and soft toys. Stafford is now
one of almost 700 branches of Clinton Cards.

NUMBER FIFTY SEVEN

    If you had walked up Greengate Street in the early
eighteenth century you would have passed The Bull and Cross
Keys on the left hand side, before you reached the market
place. It was an old timber-framed building with large
cellars that dated back to medieval times and showed that a
substantial building had stood on the site for many years.
No pictures of it have survived so that no details of its
appearance are known. Its history has to be unravelled from
Land Tax assessments, lists of chamberlains' rents, scraps
of information in a newspaper report of a talk by Philip
Dale in November 1927 and nineteenth century references to
earlier years in a bundle of papers now in the County
Record Office. (D627/4/2/5/1)

    Thomas Nicholls was sworn in as a burgess in October
1711 and, about the same time, bought John Winter's house
in Greengate Street. Nicholls was a man of some standing
since he was elected as one of the town's common council
on the day he became a burgess and was chosen as mayor in
1724 It was probably he who converted the house into an
inn with the sign of The Bull and Cross Keys. When he died
the inn was inherited by his son William and then by Mrs
Nicholls, probably William's widow. About 1758 she let
the inn to Thomas Dawson and in 1765 sold the freehold to
Thomas Ridgeway. Ridgeway continued Dawson's tenancy and
after Dawson died his widow continued to manage the inn
until about 1770, when she bought the freehold from Thomas
Ridgeway. She let the premises to Thomas Hancox. About this
time the inn closed and the building reverted to being a
private house.

    In 1785 Mrs Dawson sold the house to Francis Brookes,
a Stafford attorney and the Town Clerk. Thomas Hancox went
on living there until 1787. The premises were then let to
Arthur Morgan, a stationer and bookseller, who converted
the ground floor into a shop. In 1795 he bought a property
in Market Square and moved his business into it.

    Soon afterwards number 57 was sold to John Hall, who
seems to have used it as his town house. Hall was a well-to-
do entrepreneur. He had made his money as one of the partners

who acted as agents for those raising money through church briefs. These were licences to make collections in churches in aid of good causes. He had also helped to finance the development of collieries and ironworks in the Black Country. He modernised the property in Greengate Street, inserting eight new sash windows into the upper floors and two bow windows on the ground floor. In April 1800 he let the property to Joseph Hall, a relative, perhaps his son.

Joseph Hall fitted up the premises as a linen and woollen drapery shop. Stock was personally selected from the London and Manchester markets and warehouses and included table linen, waistcoat and breeches pieces, veils, printed muslins and calicoes priced at from two shillings and three pence to five shillings a yard. Genuine Indian muslin was also stocked at prices up to 30 shillings a yard according to its fineness. As well as his retail shop, Hall also supplied travelling chapmen and country shopkeepers with a limited trade. His prices were comparable with those charged in London and Manchester and he also offered credit.

Joseph's brother Omar also lived at number 57. He had been living at Milford before he came to Stafford. In 1797 when he was just 21 years of age, he had carried an 18 year old heiress from Milford off to London, where they had been married at St Martin's church. His bride brought a dowry which included the reversion of the Horn and Trumpet inn at Radford and of a house in Greengate Street, after the death of a relative, John Hughes.

Omar was always a finacier rather than a tradesman. By 1802 he had established a bank, with his brother as a partner. He provided credit for tradesmen, discounted bills drawn on other banks, offered a good rate of interest for money left on deposit, and issued his own £1 notes, which the Halls guaranteed to exchange for cash on demand. The bank and drapery shop shared premises. Omar was trusted by people in the town and, soon after his bank opened, he was chosen as one of the town's capital burgesses.

He invested money in the expanding coal industry of the Black Country. He and John Hall were both members of a

partnership that took over and developed Goscote colliery
and ironworks north of Walsall. In Stafford, he was the
chief promoter of schemes to bring cheaper coal to the town.
When the Staffordshire and Worcestershire canal had been
built it by-passed Stafford. A wharf for unloading coal was
built at Radford, the canal's nearest point to the town.
A scheme to build a branch canal with aquaducts over the
rivers Sow and Penk had been abandoned because of the cost.
Omar believed that a 1½ mile long tramway from Radford to
near the Green Bridge in Stafford, operated with horse-
drawn wagons, would make a substantial profit as well as
delivering cheaper coal to the town. The capital needed
to build and operate the tramway was £3,200. Omar provided
half of this sum, John Hall a quarter and John Brown, the
owner of the coal wharf near the Green Bridge, the other
quarter. Omar negotiated wayleaves to allow the tramway to
be constructed alongside the main road from Radford to
Stafford. The first load of coal was hauled on the tramway
on 1 November 1805 and 'occasioned a good deal of rejoicing
in the town'. Omar and his partners also built new lime-
kilns at Radford to add to the traffic on the tramway.
     By 1806 Joseph Hall's drapery shop was in financial
difficulties and he withdrew from the bank to use what
capital he had to save his business. However, in 1807 he
was unable to pay all his critors and was declared
bankrupt. The lease of the premises and all his stock were
advertised for sale in September1807 and were bought by
Thomas Thompson, who continued the drapery business there
in partnership with a Mr Jennings. Omar Hall and his bank
had to move out. He found new premises at 42 Greengate
Street, which belonged to his wife's relative John Hughes.
     Thomas Thompson carried on the business until he retired
in 1820, by which time he had also acquired the freehold of
the premises. In 1820 he transferred the business to his
son Thomas junior. He carried it on for only two years before
selling the premises to George Webb, a draper and silk
mercer. By that time several ground floor rooms had been
made into one large shop 31½ feet by 22 feet. This was lit
by two bow windows either side of a central door. At the

rear were a warehouse, package room, kitchen and yard with
a stable for three horses. On the first floor was a large
stock room, together with the parlour and bedroom, where
George Webb lived. There were further bedrooms on the top
floor. Twice each year the proprietor would visit warehouses in London and Manchester to select his spring and
autumn stock. Webb's son joined his father in the business
but, in 1845, they decided to close the shop, sell off the
stock and put the premises up for sale.

They were bought by Charles Morgan, who paid £1,600 for
what was soon to be numbered 57 Greengate Street. His father
Thomas Morgan, a wine and brandy merchant in the town since
1806, had taken Charles into partnership in the early 1820s
and retired in 1827. Charles Morgan was one of the first
tradesmen not to live over their business premises. His home
was further down Greengate Street and he continued to live
there after he bought number 57. He had invested wisely in
early railway shares and become a wealthy man.

When he bought Webb's premises, his intention was to
take down the old shop and rebuild it as wine vaults. The
cellars were lined in brick and refloored in readiness for
storing wine there. The front of the building was completely
rebuilt. The new elevation facing Greengate Street was
unusual in that the ground floor did not have large display
windows. The earliest picture of the new building, engraved
in 1859, shows the property with distinctive projecting
first floor windows. Above the ground floor, the building
has remained substantially unchanged externally since 1848.

Morgan's new wine vaults opened in August 1848. He
advertised that he would cultivate the family trade, carry
stocks of port, sherry, madeira, marsala, etc, in kegs, and
imported wine in bottles. Single bottles could be bought
at the counter. Special terms were vailable for larger
purchases.

Morgan's wine vaults were a feature of Greengate Street
for the next 115 years. For much of that time the Morgan
family were active in local affairs. Charles Morgan, a
town councillor for many years, served as mayor in 1845, and

Number 57 Greengate Street
and neighbouring premises.

(a) in 1859 - on the right

(b) in 1910 - below.

made the Guildhall possible by selling the site to the
County magistrates with no profit to himself. His younger
son became a well known solicitor and his elder son, John,
took over his father's business. John was chosen as mayor
in 1866. He had a particular interest in education and was
the first chairman of the newly formed Stafford School
Board in 1871, a position he held for the next 21 years. In

the twentieth century the business became a limited company
with John's son Conway, as its chairman and managing director.
Conway Morgan had joined the company after studying at Heidel-
berg University. He was an allround sportsman - Secretary of
Stafford Golf Club from 1891-8, organiser of the annual Staffordshire Lawn Tennis Championships when they were held in the
grounds of Coton Hill Hospital, President of Stafford Hockey
Club. He was the Midland Counties Lawn Tennis Champion in
1885. As a town councillor he did much to promote the laying
out of Victoria Park. His eldest son joined the Royal Navy,
was present at the Battle of Jutland in 1916 and rose to be
an Admiral. When Conway died in 1924, the family business
was taken over by Mrs Jupp, Thomas Morgan's great-great-
granddaughter.

   In May 1963 the business was sold to the Hanley based
wine merchants, G & T Munro & Co, who kept it open for four
years before the premises were leased to Hilton's Shoes Ltd
After extensive refitting of the ground floor, the shop
became one of their chain of shoe shops as Hilton's and
later as Oliver's. The shoe shop closed in 1994.

   The premises were temporarily occupied by King's Dis-
count stationery shop before becoming Ottakar's bookshop
in 1996. In 2006 Ottakar's was taken over by the larger
Waterstone's booksellers. After refitting, the new name
appeared above the shop in late October 2006.

FIFTY SEVEN A

When Charles Morgan rebuilt number 57 in 1846/8, he had
no intention of living on the premises as almost all other
shopkeepers did. The upper floors were built as offices with
a separate entrance and staircase at the side of the shop.
These upstairs premises were known as 57A.

The first tenant is not known with certainty, but was
probably Henry Ward, the county architect, In January 1863
Robert Griffith, newly appointed county architect in succession
to Henry Ward, moved into the premises.

Robert Griffith, born in 1825, had been apprenticed to
Pountney Smith, a Shrewsbury architect, but did not complete
his apprenticeship because of ill health. He then joined his
cousins J. and E.F. Griffith, builders and architects, at Quat-
ford. In the 1850s he set up in business for himself at
Bridgnorth and moved to Stafford in 1863 when he was appointed
Staffordshire County Architect. He retained a large private
practice, designing a number of asylums and churches as well
as other buildings. In Stafford, he took over the restoration
of St Chad's church after the death of Sir G. Gilbert Scott
and restored Seighford Hall. He built himself a large house,
Highfield Grove, on the west side of Wolverhampton Road in
the 1870s and died there in 1888. He was a genial, hearty
man with a strong practical bent. He had a great interest
in art and had a gallery of pictures at Highfield Grove.

After his death, 57A was let to James Moncur, road
surveyor, until 1900 and then to Richard Nevitt, surveyor
and house agent, who remained until 1908. From 1908 to about
1918 J.E.Fernie, an accountant, had an office at 57A, but
the principal tenants were Samuel Watson and Charles Owen,
a newly formed solicitors partnership, who moved in in March
1908 and stayed until the 1960s.

From the 1960s to 2000 57A was the office of George
Myatt & Co, insurance agent, and is now the office of Warren
Hill, insurance brokers.

NUMBER FIFTY EIGHT

This was still a timber-framed house in the early
eighteenth century. In 1729 it was the home of Thomas King-
stone, junior. His father, Thomas senior, had also lived
in a house in Greengate Street but we cannot be sure that
it was the same house. In 1730 Thomas junior sold his
property to Richard Mountford. Mountford had bought the
house as an investment and in the 1730s left it to be managed by Mrs Morrey. The house was rented to Thomas Spicer
and, later, to Thomas Smith. In 1757 Richard Mountford sold
the house to James Eaton junior, who continued to let it
to Thomas Smith's widow. After her death, he let it to
-- Loveliss and later to John Venables, who was living in it
in 1770 when the property was sold to Thomas Ward.

Ward died in 1784. After being in the possession of
Matthew Ward for a short time, the property was inherited
by Thomas Ward's son, Thomas junior. Both Matthew and
Thomas junior seem to have lived in part of the property
and let the rest to John Venables - perhaps as a lock-up
workshop or shop - until he left in 1787.

About this time the old house was demolished and replaced by the plain, three-storey brick building that is
there today (see page 56). Ovens for a bakery were built
at the rear of the premises and most of the ground floor
fitted out as a shop. The first tenant of the rebuilt
premises was William Thompson, a baker and confectioner,
who remained until about 1808. After he left, the bakery
was carried on by Thomas Ward Pemberton until 1829.

In 1829 the business, and probably the freehold of
the premises, were acquired by Thomas Woolley, baker, confectioner and dealer in flour. Some time later he opened
a second shop in Market Street selling ironmongery, brass
and tinned ware.. The second shop proved to be the more
profitable of the two and in September 1851 he sold the
Greengate Street shop and moved into Market Street

The new owner of number 58 was Richard Ash, who had
been renting a small grocery shop in Gaol Square since the

1820s. When he moved into number 58, he successfully combined
grocery and tea dealing with a bakery and confectioner's for
the next 37 years. When he retired in March 1866, his stock
of flour and shop fittings were offered for sale at auction.
Many of the lots were bought by John Wallis, who also became
the tenant of the shop and carried on a similar grocery, bakery and confectionery business there until the early 1870s.

By 1876 Henry Ball had taken over the premises and the
business. He died about 1880 and his widow Sarah, helped by
her son Henry junior, carried on the business. After his
mother's death in 1891, Henry carried on as Ball & Co until
1898. He then sold the business to Thomas Bunn, who remained
there until 1906.

In 1906 Mrs Mary Jenkinson, a widow, sold her shop in
Gaolgate Street and bought number 58 as a grocery and confectionery shop. She had her own special chair at the back
of the shop and, whenever the shop was open, sat there with
a lace cap on her head, supervising all that was going on.
In 1913 she sold the business to R.J.Young, who continued
to trade as Jenkinson's. In March 1921 he expanded the
business by adding a cafe serving luncheons and teas. This
became very popular and in 1932 he bought number 56 Greengate Street and transferred the cafe to the new shop, where
there was more space. Number 58 remained open as a grocery
and confectionery shop.

By 1953 the shop had been inherited by R.J.Young's
daughter, Mrs Dean. She appointed Graham Evans as manager
and gave him a fairly free hand to run the shop. Mr Evans,
a Shropshire man, had been apprenticed to a grocer in Much
Wenlock. After war-time service with the R.A.O.C., he had
worked in grocery shops in Wolverhampton and Yardley before
coming to Stafford in 1953. At that time grocers still had
to use their expertise to select much of their stock. Mr
Evans took particular care in choosing farmhouse cheeses
and Danish bacon, huge sides of which were hung on an upper
floor. Mr Evans took great pride and care in displaying
these and other groceries in the shop window.   His delicat-
essen counter attracted customers at a time when war-time

shortages had not entirely disappeared. Hams were cooked on the premises and a variety of salamis stocked. He was an expert on wine at a time when people drank it only occasionally and his advice was often sought. During the war he had picked up a knowledge of Polish and this attracted the large number of Poles who had settled round the town in post-war years.

Major alterations to the shop were made in 1969. New shop windows were put in and space at the rear taken into the shop. The bakery was moved to an upper floor.

Jenkinson's closed in the early 1980s, when the shop was taken over by Taylor's (Cannock) Bakeries as a bakery and confectioners. The company carried on the shop until 1994, when it became one of a chain of shops trading as The Bakers Oven. Number 58 has been a baker's shop continuously for over 200 years.

PRINCIPAL SOURCES

Local and County Directories 1783-1970

Roxburgh: Stafford-Know Your Town (1948)

Kemp: Freemen of Stafford Borough 1100-1997 (1998)

Staffordshire Advertiser

Stafford Newsletter

Stafford chamberlains' rents 1699-1704 and 1729-1835 (SRO
    D(W) 0/8/2-3, D1033/1, D1323/E/2)

Land Tax Assessments 1765 - 1832 with many gaps (WSL
    7/00/87-9; SRO QRP/1)

Stafford Poor Rate 1768 (WSL 7/00/86)

Census enumerators' books 1841-1901.

Map of Stafford in 1788 (Brit Museum Egerton 2872)

Ordnance Survey 1/500 map of Stafford 1881 (survey 1879)

Goad Maps from 1969

Ellerton's commonplace book (WSL 77/45) for numbers 50-2

ADDITIONAL SOURCES FOR THE HIGH HOUSE

F. Sheridan : The Ancient High House; Take a Walk through
    history.

F.W.B. Charles; Survey Report on The High House (1975)

W.Pitt: Topographical History of Staffordshire p294

White: Gazeteer and Directory of Staffordshire 1851 p 323

W.Jones: notes on the High House (WSL 7/00/4)

Ferneyhough drawings of The High House (WSL SMS370ii, 371iv)

J. Buckler drawings 1841 and 1845 (WSL)

Wills of Richard Dorrington 1596 and John Dorrington 1589
    (Public Record Office)

St Mary's Parish Register 1559-1671 (Staffs Parish Reg. Soc.)

Pennington and Rootes: The Parliamentary Committee at
    Stafford, 1643-5 (SHC 4th series Vol 1)

Copies Stafford town rents, accounts, etc in the seventeenth
    century (WSL 402)

ADDITIONAL SOURCES FOR OMAR HALL

S. Broadbridge: Communications with canals in the Stafford
    Area (Staffs Ind. Arch. Journal Vol 1)

Dawes & Ward-Perkins: Country Banks of England & Wales
    Vol 2 (2000)

ABBREVIATIONS: WSL - William Salt Library; SRO-Staffordshire
    County Record Office.

THE STAFFORD STREET SERIES   £4.99

Each book in the series relates the history of a small group of properties in the main streets of Stafford since 1700, or earlier, and gives some account of those who have occupied them. The accounts are based on research, much of which has not been published before.

Books are available from bookshops in Stafford or direct from the publisher. Numbers 2, 3 and 4 are currently out of print and stocks of number 5 are limited.

1   From High House to Bakers Oven (second, revised edition)
     ISBN 978-0-9553807-4-7

2   The Swan and its Neighbours

3   Half Way Round the Market Square

4   Into Gaolgate Street

5   Another Side to Market Square
     ISBN 978-0-9553807-0-9

6   From Crabbery Street to Lewis' Lane
     ISBN 978-0-9553807-1-6

7   Round the Corner of Greengate Street
     ISBN 978-0-9553807-2-3

8   The Bear and its Neighbours
     ISBN 978-0-9553807-3-0

Published by ROY LEWIS BOOKS, 8 Tamar Grove, Stafford ST17 9SL

Greengate.

Stafford.

£4.99

ISBN 978-0-9553807-4-7